LIGHT FROM PARIS

Light from Paris

CARDINAL LUSTIGER ON FAITH
AND CONTEMPORARY CULTURE

Gerald Hanratty

FOUR COURTS PRESS

Set in 11 on 13 Times New Roman
and published by

FOUR COURTS PRESS LTD
Kill Lane, Blackrock, Co. Dublin, Ireland

and in North America by

FOUR COURTS PRESS LTD
c/o International Specialized Book Services,
5804 NE Hassalo Street, Portland, OR 97213.

A catalogue record for this title
is available from the British Library.

ISBN I-85I82-184-8

Printed in Ireland
by ßetaprint Ltd, Dublin.

CONTENTS

LIFE AND DIFFICULT TIMES

During a homily on the occasion of the fortieth anniversary of the liberation of Paris Cardinal Jean-Marie Lustiger recalled the heroic witness of those who upheld basic human and Christian values during the occupation of France. Among those who resisted the almost overwhelming propaganda of the time and risked their lives in the elaboration and dissemination of a critical response to the inhuman National Socialist ideology was the theologian Henri de Lubac, who was present in the cathedral. De Lubac had argued in the clandestinely circulated journal of the Christian resistance that the real significance of the horrendous events of the war and occupation would be overlooked if they were confined within political or national horizons. Instead, these events had to be seen as particularly tragic episodes in the universal context of the spiritual drama of humanity. And, as Lustiger also recalled in his homily, de Lubac had insisted during the final stages of the war that victory would be hollow unless the evil spirits of hatred and vengeance were exorcised. Even more fundamental, according to de Lubac, were the spiritual and moral issues involved in the widespread surrender to one of the principal temptations of the age – contempt for human beings.

Towards the end of his homily Lustiger referred to another edition of the journal of the Christian resistance which had been distributed from Lyons in 1942 by de Lubac and his Jesuit colleagues Gaston Fessard and Pierre Chaillet. In a compact text the authors affirmed that every human being is the bearer of an inalienable dignity and freedom; there are sacred personal rights which are not subject to the coercive authority of the nation or the state or any political power. The primordial God-given rights to life, truth, justice and love had been suppressed by the adherents of an amoral and idolatrous ideology. Nevertheless, truth would prevail over lies, idolatry and violence; love would overcome hatred. There is one faith on earth which engendered and protected these truths, and one Church which continues to proclaim them, the authors declared in their urgent appeal for resistance.

[7]

As Archbishop of Paris, Lustiger brings a similarly forthright and incisive approach to the roles of pastor, teacher, apologist, and commentator on social and cultural trends. In articles, lectures, homilies, interviews and broadcasts he has addressed the spiritual, intellectual and moral dilemmas of the closing decades of the century with candour and courage. Predictably, his reflections often bear the marks of French conditions and occasions. But they also cast unexpected light into many corners of contemporary western culture. Even more importantly, they are a persuasive apologia for the universal significance and perennial fruitfulness of biblical and Christian revelation.[1]

Lustiger's distinctive spiritual history, his exposure to twentieth-century barbarism, his varied pastoral experience and extensive knowledge of the influences moulding contemporary European culture, enhance the authority of his reflections. Born in Paris in 1926 to immigrant Jewish parents, he received his early education in state schools which nevertheless transmitted inescapable impressions of the pivotal role of the Christian faith in French history and tradition. On reading the Bible at the age of ten, Lustiger intuitively linked the passion of the New Testament Messiah with the sufferings of Israel and the ordeals of the Jewish people throughout history. Even at this stage he discerned a continuity between the two Testaments and found nothing to offend his Jewish sensibilities or justify anti-Semitic prejudices. The Christian witness of French acquaintances and friends, and more crucially of his host family in Germany during the summers of 1936 and 1937, intensified Lustiger's youthful curiosity and fascination with the biblical responses to the fundamental questions concerning origins and destinies, life and death, good and evil, salvation and loss.

While Lustiger is understandably reticent about some of his wartime experiences, he has given a restrained account of the events and experiences which were decisive for his future course. Having been transferred to Orleans by his parents at the outset of the war, he was favourably impressed once more by the charity and discretion of his host family and those who befriended him. As he reflected on the agonising issues of the time, he was increasingly attracted by the Gospels and by a classic of the French spiritual tradition – the apologia of Blaise Pascal. Lustiger was inexorably drawn towards the Messiah of Israel, whom he now saw as the fulfilment of God's promises to his people and the One who illuminated the dark mystery of evil and the scandal of suffering. Two unplanned visits to Orleans cathedral on Holy Thursday and Good Friday in 1940 sealed his resolve to seek Baptism. A thorough catechesis and investigation of Christian origins deepened his convictions that Christianity was the harvest of Judaism and that conversion did not entail a repudiation of his Jewish identity.

The years of Lustiger's Christian initiation coincided with the most formidable ordeals of his life. There was the distress caused by his parents' inability to comprehend or countenance his option for Christianity. The betrayal, arrest and removal of his mother to the Parisian transit camp of Drancy in 1942 was even more painful. Almost forty years later a detailed history of the fates of French Jews during the occupation revealed the day and the number of the convoy on which she departed for Auschwitz in 1943. Lustiger's own position became more precarious as the political and military situation deteriorated. Carrying false identity papers, he escaped from occupied Orleans and was reunited with his father in a coal-mining district where they lived in a 'kind of brutal fraternity' of displaced persons, revolutionaries and anarchists. In these harsh conditions he entered adult life as 'a worker with a pay slip and a ration card for tobacco'. Once more, however, an extension of the anti-Semitic net necessitated a sudden departure. On this occasion, the Christian resistance provided false identity papers and enabled Lustiger to find employment for his father in a Jesuit agricultural school and his own final wartime refuge in the Toulouse region.

Lustiger's wartime ordeals were aggravated by the profoundly disillusioning experience of the French *débacle*. As a child of parents who inculcated reverence for the civic, political, cultural and educational traditions of their adopted homeland, he was shocked by the dramatic military collapse, the widespread indifference to the basic values of truth and justice, and the capitulation to racist propaganda. The abject failure of large sections of the academic and cultural élites was another disconcerting feature of wartime France. Lustiger's own faith was buttressed by the life-saving practical assistance he and others received from the Christian resistance and by the uncompromising declarations of such notable figures as Archbishops Saliège and Gerlier, the Lyons Jesuits, the Swiss theologian Charles Journet, and the historian Henri Marrou. At the end of the war Lustiger was nauseated again by the savage reprisals and unbridled excesses which he witnessed on the streets of Toulouse. The hatred and violence unleashed by the war could only be endured in the light of a faith which entrusted everything to God who revealed himself in the redemptive passion and death of the Messiah. In view of Lustiger's wartime experiences, it is not surprising that his reflections on the cultural climate of the century were frequently concerned with the ideological currents which gave rise to murderous totalitarian regimes and with the bankruptcy of the European intelligentsia when confronted with spiritual, intellectual and moral crises.

Memories of the barbarism which he witnessed during the war – and of the example of those who spoke and lived the truth, at whatever cost – strengthened Lustiger's resolve to commit himself to Christ's redemptive mission in the priesthood. His student years in the Sorbonne, the Institut Catholique and the Paris seminary were marked therefore by the inevitable postwar ferment in French Catholicism. As an enthusiastic participant in student organisations, Lustiger took part in impassioned debates on the political implications of the Gospel and the role of religious commitment in the construction of a just society. Although he supported the 'party of progress', his exposure to tyranny and the influence of thinkers such as Jacques Maritain and Raymond Aron delivered him from one of the most insidious temptations of the time – the construction of an ideal communist society which would encompass the totality of human existence and solve the riddle of history.

On the spiritual and theological planes, the renewal of biblical, patristic and liturgical studies was particularly significant. From Lustiger's perspective, the initiatives inspired by Louis Bouyer, Henri de Lubac and Jean Daniélou represented an authentic pastoral zeal, an ecumenical spirit and a refreshing openness to contemporary thought. Because these scholars aimed to recover and render accessible the submerged riches of the Christian tradition, they transcended the sterile controversies between progressives and conservatives in the French Church. Not surprisingly, Bouyer's emphasis on the historical continuity of the Old and New Testaments and on the links between Jewish and Christian liturgies was a congenial development. On the much-debated question of a Christian philosophy, on the relations between modern culture and the Christian tradition, and on the means to effect a spiritual and intellectual renewal in the Church, de Lubac was the most reliable guide. For his part Daniélou combined the highest standards in patristic scholarship with a vigorous apostolate to the university community. During Lustiger's student years, the Parisian environment also provided outstanding opportunities for the discovery of art and for reflection on the spiritual and cultural significance of modern artistic movements.

As chaplain to the Sorbonne and other university institutions for fifteen years (1954-69), Lustiger was engaged in an apostolate which exhilarated and fascinated him. In this role he shared a community life in which personal preferences were subordinated to the common task of fostering the lay Christian vocation. The university was seen as an appropriate setting for the emergence of a renewed missionary Church in which the joy of responding to God's gift and the beauty of a Christian community would be manifest. The university environment also ensured that Lustiger was frequently challenged by questions concerning the relationship of faith to the achievements of reason in the rapidly changing fields of secular learning. In the volatile political climate of the time there was the further challenge of bringing the reconciling spirit of the Gospel to bear on the divisive issues in French society, most notably the Algerian war and the emergence of irrational revolutionary fervour in 1968. Ministry in the university also afforded numerous opportunities for encounters and dialogues with non-Christian religions and for consideration of the phenomena of unbelief and indifference in a culture which had been profoundly influenced by Christian revelation.

Lustiger's faith in the perennial fruitfulness of the Gospel and his commitment to the mission of the Church were strengthened by the vigorous apostolate in the Sorbonne. In a secularist and sometimes hostile environment he accompanied numerous artists, intellectuals and students on their journey to faith. Moreover, the theological perspectives, pastoral strategies and ecumenical spirit of the chaplaincy were endorsed by the Vatican Council. But his final years in the Sorbonne were nevertheless marred by unexpected trials. In the light of Lustiger's own experience of totalitarianism, he was repelled by the intellectual tyranny, demagoguery and utopian fantasies of the student revolutionaries and their accomplices in cultural and academic circles. At the same time, irresponsible and destructive attitudes, which seemed to reflect the fanaticism of the student revolutionaries, emerged in the post-conciliar Church. Lustiger was scandalised by demands for the abandonment of a visible Christian identity and by corrosive criticism of the sacramental and institutional dimensions of the Church. These attitudes represented a betrayal of the Council and an abdication of memory and reason.

It was in an unsettled ecclesiastical climate, therefore, that Lustiger departed from 'the privileged but isolated canton of French intellect-ual life' for a distant suburban parish. Ministry in the more sedate and tradition-bound environment of a parish contrasted sharply with the animated surroundings of the Sorbonne. And since the significance of the priesthood and of parish ministry were being questioned, Lustiger had to reflect once more on the nature and methods of evangelisation in an impersonal urban environment. Drawing on his own experience and observation he concluded that the Sunday parish liturgy – and the divine action in the other sacraments – would be the axis on which his ministry was based. The decision to make the Sunday Mass a privileged time, rich in meaning, joy and spiritual beauty bore fruit as parishioners from different ethnic and social backgrounds formed a more committed and united community. Parish ministry, Lustiger soon realised, was as challenging and invigorating as the Sorbonne chaplaincy. In this setting too he could exercise the essential priestly ministry of 'giving spiritual birth to God's children'. He also had opportunities for a disciplined study of Scripture, an exploration of the history and significance of Judaism, and a more reflective study of theology, represented especially by the works of Hans Urs von Balthasar. Christian faith, Lustiger concluded, could still be an agent of transformation in all areas of life. But as salvation history – from the Sinai desert to the martyrs of Korea – testified, fidelity to the Word invariably encountered opposition and entailed sacrifice, even to the shedding of blood. In this, as in every generation, the vocation of the children of God was to remain faithful to the Light and 'attest that God loves the world and that the world is not lost or left alone with its nothingness'.

After ten years of parish ministry Lustiger could only interpret his return to Orleans as bishop in terms of a providential divine endorsement of his life and vocation. His personal history encompassed, of course, the earlier sojourn in the city as a refugee and outcast from the fatherland, the decisive encounter with the mystery of the suffering Messiah in the cathedral and the indelible impression of a tall Senghalese soldier giving his life in defence of the city. Lustiger saw the rich symbolism of the ordination liturgy on the Feast of the Immaculate Conception as a résumé of salvation history. It included the accounts of cosmic and human origins from the Book of Genesis and of the reconciliation of pagans with the chosen people through the Cross of Christ from the Epistle to the Ephesians. The history and grace of salvation were concentrated, in turn, in the figure of the virgin mother and daughter of Zion; because Mary believed and submitted to God's will, she received in advance the new life given in Christ and perpetuated in the universal mission of the Church.

Lustiger's motto – that 'everything is possible to God' – seemed even more appropriate when, fifteen months after his arrival in Orleans, he was transferred to Paris. Again, the liturgical feast of the day on which he learned of his transfer was an appropriate spiritual context and resounded with biblical hope. In the Presentation of Jesus in the Temple, Mary appeared as 'the hope of a transfigured humanity for the nations as well as for Israel'. The elderly figures of Simeon and Anna were in the line of Israel's prophets, while Simeon's address to Mary proclaimed the suffering Messiah and Redeemer of the world and indicated that, like Mary, all the disciples of Christ are called to share in his Passion. In the light of the Presentation, Lustiger could see that, despite the almost impossible mission which awaited him, he was following a logic of faith and obedience to divine providence.

ATHEISM WITHIN CHRISTIANITY

Following a hermeneutic line enunciated by de Lubac, Lustiger insists that the atheistic and secular strands in modern Western culture cannot be understood without reference to the Judaeo-Christian matrix from which they emerged. The atheism, agnosticism and religious indifference in Western societies have to be seen as components of a profound crisis in a culture which has been indelibly marked by divine revelation. This paradoxical conclusion follows from what Lustiger sees as incontrovertible historical evidence.

In the context of world history, biblical revelation represents a completely original perspective on the fundamental questions of the origin and goal of existence. From the beginning of revelation God presents himself as the transcendent and universal cause or Creator of all things; the biblical God, unlike the gods of the mythologies, is distinct from the world which he creates and upholds. For their part, human beings receive an astonishing dignity and freedom from their creation in God's image and likeness and an exalted status in the intelligible universe which is committed to them. The universalism of the creation narrative is reinforced in the divine promise to Abraham that 'all the nations of the earth will be blessed'. This universalism and hope of salvation for all the nations are proclaimed again by Israel's prophets and culminate in the incarnation of the Son and Messiah who is the Light of all peoples. At the Passover celebration or Last Supper, Jesus opens the gates of Israel's memory and admits pagans to the hope inscribed in the Covenant with the chosen people. The unrestricted scope of salvation is ratified when Jesus, associating himself with Isaiah's prophecy, promises that his blood of the Covenant will be shed 'for all'. Again, the gift of the Spirit at Pentecost establishes a new assembly of Jews and those who were pagans and endorses the salvific mission of the Church to all nations. Finally, the Revelation of St John envisages a Church in which racial, national, cultural and linguistic differences are transcended in 'a great multitude which no man could number, from every nation, from all tribes and peoples and tongues'.

Lustiger has no doubt that the extension of Western civilisation to all parts of the earth is due to the univeralism which is an intrinsic

feature of biblical revelation. The only other explanation for the
pervasive influence of Western civilisation is that of the modern
race theorists – the essential superiority of white-skinned people.
Lustiger points to the fact that it was the universal standpoint inherited
by the West which led to the discovery and exploration of all parts
of the world. In another key, modern science, technology and
communications, and their deployment throughout the world, are
inconceivable without the universal biblical horizon and the exalted
status given to human beings in the creation. Likewise, the ideas of
human equality, a universal law and democracy, could only emerge
from a cultural matrix which traced the origins of humanity to a
common Creator and Lord. Lustiger acknowledges the substantial
contribution of the Greek and Latin cultures to the conceptual, legal,
scientific and technical virtuosity of the west. But it was nevertheless
the providential encounter with Judaeo-Christianity which expanded
Graeco-Roman horizons and elevated the Greek philosophers'
discovery of reason to the universal standpoint.

According to Lustiger, the successive waves of secular and
atheistic thought which have emerged in modern Western culture
must be interpreted in the light of the singular gifts received through
biblical revelation. The varieties of unbelief and rejection of God
are the 'temptations', ' risks' and even 'perversions' of individuals
and peoples who have been exposed to biblical revelation and
experienced the concomitant liberation of human reason. It is significant, therefore, that Western atheism invariably portrays itself in
terms of a negation of the Judaeo-Christian God. Consideration of
the secularism and unbelief in Western culture leads therefore to the
paradoxical conclusions on which Lustiger insists – that 'atheistic
society is Christian society' and 'atheistic rationalism is nothing
other than the temptation or trial of a believer'.

To believe in God today, Lustiger argues in another provocative
thesis, is to follow the same demanding spiritual, intellectual and
moral path as Abraham, who is our father in faith. Furthermore,
although modern and contemporary atheism presents itself in varied
and apparently novel guises, the Bible actually contains a complete
typology of the strands of unbelief and rejection of God which have
emerged in Western culture. Thus the original biblical sin of pride,
or the refusal to acknowledge the contingency of existence and
acquiesce in the limits of the human condition, anticipates a pervasive
strand in modern Western atheism. The extravagant ambition to

construct the tower of Babel prefigures the recurring modern Promethean challenge to God's sovereignty and the temptation to usurp the divine prerogatives of absolute knowledge, power and freedom. In another key, the numerous Old Testament condemnations of idolatry can be seen as admonitions against the divinisation of intramundane realities in successive ideologies. The Wisdom of Solomon, for instance, traces the 'corruption of life' to the fabrication of 'futile' or 'counterfeit' gods from earthly clay. Solomon anticipates, therefore, the rationalist and utilitarian ideologies which give rise to a parallel corruption of life through the ascription of absolute value to the instruments and products of reason or the objects of human desire.

The New Testament accounts of Christ's temptations also yield a diagnostic framework for the identification of Western ideological deviations. The first temptation, in which Satan promises dominion over the whole earth, identifies the motivation of the ideologies which are based on an unlimited will to power over territories and peoples. The second temptation, in which Christ is invited to change stones into bread, corresponds to the totalitarian perversion of reason which claims to be the sole measure and becomes murderous and even suicidal. According to Lustiger, the third temptation encompasses the others and engenders the greatest atrocities. When Christ refuses to vindicate his divine status by throwing himself from the pinnacle of the Temple, he anticipates and warns against the pathological ambition to fabricate a 'new' or 'super' humanity. The twentieth-century ideologies, which consigned individuals and peoples to an inferior or sub-human status, subverted the indispensable patrimony of biblical universalism and the foundations on which the dignity, value and equality of all human beings are based.

Following de Lubac again, Lustiger believes that the successive modern waves of atheistic thought represent an unprecedented spiritual crisis or drama in Western culture. From the biblical perspective, it is clear, of course, that atheism and idolatry are permanent possibilities in the lives of individuals and societies and that human imperfection and inconstancy ensure that evangelisation can never be complete or irreversible. However, Lustiger finds the earliest intimations of modern Promethean atheism in late-medieval Nominalist theology which portrayed the relationship between God and human beings in conflictual terms. This decadent theology misconceived the Christian vision of God as loving Creator and cooperator through grace with human freedom. The Nominalist conception of God as an omnipotent and arbitrary will, which demeaned human freedom and dignity, was the remote ancestor of modern rebellious atheism which excludes God in the name of untrammelled human autonomy. But the splintering of Christianity during the Reformation and the associated religious wars, the sceptical crisis of the post-Reformation period, the assertive humanism of the Renaissance, the extravagant expectations evoked by the scientific and technological revolutions, and the emergence of a secular and libertine mentality in France, contributed to the formation of a cultural climate favourable to atheism.

The confluence of these currents in the seventeenth and eighteenth centuries gave rise to what Lustiger sees as the 'spiritual crisis' or 'internal schism' of modern Western culture. With an unquestioning faith in progress, enlightenment and modernity, the leading thinkers of the time embarked on a radical and destructive critique of the religious, philosophical and moral foundations of the Western tradition. Lustiger is convinced, however, that the most pernicious development was the eighteenth-century Enlightenment's conception of autonomous and self-sufficient reason. Abandoning the venerable religious and philosophical insight that human reason is not its own measure, the advanced thinkers proclaimed that reason could establish its own goals and rely on its own resources to achieve them. In the name of emancipated and sceptical reason, they consigned the venerable questions of the origin and end of existence to the oblivion of an earlier immature stage of human development. The Enlightenment project recklessly ignored human limitations and exalted reason in its scientific, technological and utilitarian applications. In the high tide of Enlightenment the atheistic undertaking presented itself in clear relief – 'the salvation of humanity by itself and the birth of a society guided by human reason alone'. But the titanic attempts to construct ideal societies actually led to the worst deviations. Drawing on the analyses of Hannah Arendt and his own direct experience, Lustiger insists that the exclusive sway of enlightened reason in social life and the attempts to construct political utopias inevitably gave rise to the totalitarian excesses. When the fanatical standard-bearers of twentieth-century ideologies refused to accept any limits to their imposition of rational programmes on society, they succumbed to the greatest perversion and contemptuously disposed of human beings. The attempts to establish social order on the basis of enlightened and unfettered human reason engendered the most irrational and barbarous atrocities.

From Lustiger's perspective, it is of course significant that modern enlightened atheism inspired the most venomous of all anti-Semitic outbreaks. The temptation, to which Christians had periodically yielded since the emergence of the Church from its Jewish matrix, became a satanic perversion in the racist ideology of the twentieth century. But the seeds of the Holocaust were sown in the works of eighteenth-century *philosophes* such as Voltaire and Diderot. Whereas the anti-Semitism of the preceding centuries stemmed from conflicting interpretations of divine revelation and salvation history, the modern variations were based on contempt for the people chosen to bear witness to God's sovereignty. What had been 'a dispute among inheritors' gave way to the murderous designs of twentieth-century atheistic totalitarians against those to whom God confided his Name and Word and the vocation of testifying to the presence of the Absolute in history.

In the final analysis, however, the murderous totalitarian systems of the twentieth century are consequences of the sinful misuse of the gifts of reason and freedom. The foundations were laid in the aggressive rationalism of the eighteenth-century *philosophes* and the even more demiurgic enterprises of their nineteenth-century successors Hegel and Marx. The all-embracing speculative system of Hegel, which subsumed and secularised Christianity, was itself the outcome of a voracious rational quest undertaken within the confines of Christian theology. Marx's inversion of Hegel's system was based on a similarly abusive use of reason in pursuit of an unattainable perfection on the social and political planes. The Marxist system, like that of National Socialism, was a concentration of all the temptations of the human spirit in search of the absolute. But however distasteful the conclusion may be, it is nevertheless true that when Hitler, Stalin, and even Pol Pot yielded to this temptation and killed indiscriminately in their uncompromising attempts to establish a perfect kingdom on earth, they remained within the orbit of Western civilisation which bears the imprint of biblical and Christian revelation.

THE SUICIDAL TEMPTATION
OF THE WEST

Lustiger acknowledges that the Holocaust and the Gulags of the twentieth century have dimmed the Enlightenment vision of a new humanity freed from evil and saved by its own resources. But facile optimism has been replaced by weary scepticism in many segments of contemporary Western societies. There is a widespread indifference to the fundamental issues of the origin and end of existence and an inability to distinguish good from evil. When the memory of an absolute ground of existence and of values recedes, human life lacks form and direction. From the standpoint of belief, this mentality has to be seen as a spiritual, intellectual and moral failure to advert to the contingency of existence and the need for healing and salvation. In these circumstances people also succumb to idolatry and even become accomplices of forces which are hostile to human life. While there is an obvious revulsion against the spectacular overt violence unleashed by the totalitarian ideologies, there is nevertheless a cultural void which, Lustiger believes, has to be classified as a 'death wish' or a 'suicidal temptation'.

One of the most insidious threats to human life arises from the exclusion of moral values from the domains of science and technology. The prodigious expansion of human control over nature has led to an idolatrous reliance on the instruments and products of pragmatic reason. But when the human body is seen in a scientifico-technological light and treated as an object which is available for experimentation and manipulation, there are ominous consequences for the transmission and protection of human life. In the development and preservation of human embryos *in vitro*, and the eventual disposal of those which are superfluous, there is a pernicious transgression of limits. The gravity of the transgression becomes more obvious as scientific evidence accumulates that each embryo, rather than being an anonymous speck of matter, is an individual human life and must therefore be accorded an unconditional respect. In Lustiger's eyes, the uncompromising stance of the Church is a balanced and salutary response to programmes which have obvious parallels with those undertaken by the notorious physicians of Auschwitz; 'the bloody eugenics of the thirties in Germany', he writes, 'find a white-gloved justification in the hospitals of 1984.'

There is further evidence of the inroads of the suicidal temptation in the practice and toleration of induced abortion. Here, as with racist and eugenic programmes, societies face a stark choice. 'Once we have ceded on the respect due to human integrity', Lustiger warns, 'we know that we shall acquiesce to everything.' But the acceptance of abortion cannot be isolated from a wider cultural context in which the idolatrous pursuit of power, possessions and pleasure is relentlessly promoted. Nietzsche's prophetic insight – that concentration on false intramundane deities inevitably gives rise to amoral nihilism – is vindicated as Western Europe presents the spectacle of unprecedentedly wealthy populations who, due to neurotic concern for their own security and survival, are almost incapable of transmitting life to new generations. In this spiritually impoverished situation, children are seen as possessions or insurance policies rather than being loved for their own sakes and received as uniquely valuable gifts of a loving Creator. No realistic assessment of the spiritual and moral climate of the West can overlook 'the death-bearing contradictions' of societies in which 'the fruitfulness of love is under attack and the fruits of love are being aborted'.

Contemporary culture is also confronted by the immense challenge posed by the mass media and the pressures exerted by ingenious techniques of marketing and publicity. In this area, too, feasibility is taken to be the only criterion so that the individual's capacity for decision and choice is suffocated by ever more sophisticated techniques of persuasion. As these techniques progressively reduce human consciousness to measurable responses, a foundational principle of Western culture – that we can distinguish between truth and uncertain opinions – is being undermined. Moreover, it is clear that the powerful techniques of marketing and publicity are being used to condition public opinion on important issues. Thus the incessant publication of the results of opinion polls, and the interpretations supplied by 'experts', facilitate the formation of a majority or dominant opinion which, in turn, becomes the standard of truth. In the absence of an intellectual and moral critique of these practices, the logic of the ever-expanding communications industry is the control of societies and their subordination to economic interests. To highlight the influence of the media and communications industries, Lustiger points to the practice of governments making decisions on the basis of evidence supplied by opinion polls. In these conditions, ethical considerations about the order or common good of societies receive scant attention. There can be little doubt either that the rapid capitulation of Western societies on the vital issue of abortion was influenced by orchestrated publicity campaigns. Finally, there are the examples of politicians who, adjusting to the demands of *Realpolitik* and media pressures to conform to the dominant opinion, 'swing from noble sentiments to craven cynicism'. The expansion of the means of communication, Lustiger believes, presents a more demanding intellectual and moral challenge to Western culture than the availability of nuclear energy.

The barbaric contempt for human life which has disfigured twentieth-century history, the inroads of the suicidal temptation, and the threats to human dignity and freedom from an idolatrous dedication to power, possessions and pleasure lead Lustiger to the conclusion that the nature of our humanity is the basic issue in contemporary Western culture. At a time when inquiries concerning the origin and purpose of existence are frequently suppressed or evoke derisory sceptical responses, there is an urgent need for a recovery of the questions, experiences and insights which gave rise to the Western concept of human nature. If we cannot reach a consensus on a common good and purpose of human life, we must admit that our existence and history are meaningless and that the 'universalism' on which our civilisation was built is illusory.

According to Lustiger, there is an urgent need for a renewed moral vision of the significance of human embodiment. When the body is artificially detached from its human matrix and treated as a morally neutral object of experimentation and manipulation, personal integrity and dignity are degraded. The relentless promotion of a hedonistic outlook, and the assumptions that sensual appetites are not subject to moral choice and that the gratification of desire is independent of the exigencies of love and fidelity, have led to a de-humanisation of interpersonal relationships and a brutalization of human behaviour. Citing maxims of Paul Ricoeur and Emmanuel Lévinas – that 'the human body is the guardian of all lived metaphors' and 'the face of the other person says to me: You shall not kill' – Lustiger argues that the Church cannot shirk the painful duty of alerting societies to the inadvisability of legalising, and thus expressing approval of, behaviour which is incompatible with human dignity and signifies complicity with the suicidal temptation. Rather than conforming to socially dominant opinions, the Church must continue to proclaim the truly 'progressive' truths which are consonant with human dignity and promote 'a superior ecology of the human body'.

THE RECOVERY OF REASON

Lustiger believes that the pervasive uncertainty about human identity and purpose in Western culture stems from a profound crisis of philosophical reason. On the one hand, there is disillusionment with the manifest failure of enlightened, atheistic and self-sufficient reason which, rather than liberating and saving humanity, gave birth to perverse and irrational totalitarian movements. But the influence of positivist and empiricist mentalities, and the prestige accorded to scientific, technological and calculating reason, have also stifled philosophical wonder, ultimate concern and moral sensibility. Because modern – and post-modern – Western culture has jettisoned much of the spiritual, intellectual and moral patrimony accumulated by generations, it 'lacks wisdom, the savour of the true and the joy of the good'.

Modern history and contemporary experience supply abundant evidence for the lethal contradictions arising from the crisis of reason. Thus the enthusiastic modern espousal of the universality and inviolability of human rights has been accompanied by cynical and widespread violations of the basic right to life. In successive modern revolutionary movements, the rights to freedom, equality and human solidarity have been invoked to justify the incarceration, torture and murder of racial minorities and others consigned to an inferior status. Likewise, the right to freedom is invoked to justify abortion, embryo research, euthanasia and the exclusion of those with mental or physical handicaps from the human family. Lustiger finds an exemplary illustration of the crisis of reason in the post-war Nuremberg trials of doctors and scientists who, in the cause of medical research, violated the human and bodily integrity of the inmates of concentration camps. Rather than basing their determinations of guilt and innocence on fundamental philosophical and moral principles, however, the Nuremberg judges could only justify their decisions by referring to the repulsive consequences of the research practices. In such a climate of uncertainty, Lustiger points out, 'we cannot know what we are permitted or forbidden to do with our bodies, what bodily integrity and individual identity actually mean.'

In the light of the gross violations of humans rights which have occurred throughout the twentieth century, the recurrent failures of cultural, academic and political élites to identify and expose these violations, and the influence of philosophical scepticism and moral relativism, Lustiger advocates an extension of historical memory beyond the ruptures of the modern age and an exploration of the original significance of philosophical reason. Only a renewal of philosophical reason through *anamnesis* or 'recollection' can establish a solid platform for the identification and defence of human rights and a consensus on a common good of humanity. 'The motherland of reason', Lustiger writes, 'is our root, our heritage, the womb from which everything was born.' But a retrieval of the motherland of reason can be achieved only through spiritual, intellectual and moral conversion. The suppression of ultimate questions, the abuse of freedom and the Promethean ambitions of modern rationality have to be seen as the sins of peoples who have perverted or failed to respond to the gifts they have received. As the journey to conversion prescribed in the Spiritual Exercises of St Ignatius of Loyola includes a recall and assessment, not only of an individual's life history but also that of the human race, so the *anamnesis* of reason requires a rediscovery and assimilation of the originating experiences and insights of Western culture.

The first fruit of *anamnesis* is a retrieval of the venerable insight that human reason is not its own measure. From the perspective of the philosophical and religious wellsprings of Western culture, the assumptions that reason can ground and explain itself, establish its own goals and be answerable to itself alone have to be seen as transgressions of the limits inscribed in human nature. A return to these wellsprings also leads to a recognition that ours is a situated rather than an absolute freedom and that the assertion of unfettered autonomy gives birth to murderous tyrannies and self-destructive narcissism. Through *anamnesis* we are led to acknowledge that our reason and freedom are not self-constituting and that 'the end to which humanity is tending cannot be produced by itself any more than it could create itself at the beginning'. The only realistic antidote to the modern crisis of reason and to the uncertainty about human identity and purpose is the restoration of an absolute horizon or finality 'which is properly unconditional and both transcends and precedes us'.

Following 'the anthropological optimism of the revealed tradition', Lustiger believes that human reason can affirm the existence of God as the origin and end of all things. But as a consideration of modern atheism and secularism shows, the search for God in Western culture inevitably encounters signposts which are marked by divine revelation. Because God is transcendent and differs radically from any idea we can form of him, we are subject to the temptations of confining God within the horizon of our mental constructs or idolatrously divinising ourselves or other intramundane realities. A purifying *anamnesis* can nevertheless bring us to a realisation that we are open to, or, in a venerable phrase, 'capable' of God. 'To believe in God', Lustiger writes, 'is for persons to open their hearts and intelligence to a purification compelling them to accept that they are not masters of the One who comes to them, and to accept that they are not their own master.' To discover – and be discovered by – the one unseen God is to find the measure of reason and the identity and purpose of every human being. The openness to the Wholly Other, or to the One who is at once deeper within and higher than the heights of each person, is of course a time-honoured theme of the philosophical and spiritual traditions. Lustiger recalls a formulation of St Gregory of Nyssa – that the rational and free human being, created in the image and likeness of God, cannot be encompassed or comprehended in a definition. And the same insight recurs in the terse apologetic aphorism of Blaise Pascal – that 'man infinitely transcends man'. To acknowledge our contingency and admit that our reason and freedom are neither completely self-constituting nor self-determining is to exalt rather than demean our humanity. From the wellsprings of our culture we learn that human dignity hinges on our relationship with a sovereign Creator and that this transcendent sacred dimension of our lives is 'the heart of human memory and hope'.

While the *anamnesis* of reason and the affirmation of God's existence sustain a hope that does not deceive, they afford no support for a naively optimistic view of human nature. That human beings have a capacity for evil, or that reason and freedom are fragile and corruptible, are inferences based on irrefutable historical evidence. In particular, the eruptions of irrational barbarism in the 'enlightened' and 'progressive' modern age compel us to face the reality of 'a tragic depth of evil, a kind of chasm in the human condition'. Availing himself again of de Lubac's analysis and drawing on his own experience, Lustiger argues that the tragedy of evil represents a spiritual drama and that redress can be found only in the spiritual traditions of humanity. In the light of our wounded natures and proclivities towards evil, the 'divine morals' of biblical and Christian revelation are the most realistic antidote to human sinfulness. A universal and redeeming rationality, which respects the uniqueness and dignity of every human being, must embrace the distinctive revealed ways of conversion, repentance, forgiveness, mercy, hope and love. These ways are concentrated, of course, in the figure of Christ, who is the new Adam, the suffering Messiah and the resurrected Son of God. But Christ is also 'the Way, the Truth and the Life', and the One who 'introduced a universal dimension in human history and healed the wounds of human reason'.

THE CHRISTIAN DIFFERENCE

Due to the imprint of divine revelation, and specifically of the Gospel, the nations of Europe form 'an historical and cultural unity'. But European – and by extension, Western – history and culture are also marked by forgetfulness and rejection of God's revelation and gift of himself and thus by what Lustiger calls 'the perverted fruits of Christianity'. Moreover, in this, as in every preceding generation, evangelisation entails a spiritual struggle against the paganism 'which characterizes every human being born in the flesh'.

The cultural soil of some areas of the West is similar in many respects, Lustiger believes, to that in which the Gospel seed was sown in ancient Rome. Today, as in ancient Rome, the light of the Gospel has to contend with the darkness of mentalities which are often sceptical, indifferent and hedonistic. Nevertheless, despite the pressures and inducements towards spiritual, intellectual and moral lethargy, Lustiger detects an increasing openness to fundamental questioning and a search for stable values in contemporary societies. Furthermore, at a time when the essential truths of faith are no longer transmitted across the generations, and the Church is not experienced as a permanent, if perhaps jaded, fixture on the social landscape, the Gospel can be proclaimed and received again in its original freshness, truth and beauty. In a climate of uncertainty about human identity and purpose, and of a lack of consensus on the foundations of human rights, Lustiger is convinced that apologetics and evangelisation must follow an anthropological path. The unique light which Christianity sheds on our humanity can be a springboard for a new evangelisation.

The first plank in the Church's insistence on the inalienable dignity and value of every human being is, of course, the unequivocal universalism of biblical revelation. Because the existence of each of us is grounded in the world-transcendent God, we can affirm – in the forthright expression of the American Declaration of Independence that 'all men are created equal ... endowed by their Creator with certain inalienable rights.' This transcendent reference, and our creation in the image and likeness of God, establish an unshakeable foundation for the dignity and rights of every member of our species. In the light of God's sovereignty, human rights are not dependent on the nation or the state or the opinion of the majority at any time or place. As witnesses to the truth that God is the ultimate guarantor of human rights, Christians have to insist, at whatever cost, that each member of the human family is of incalculable value and should never be subject to idolatrous tyrannies in which Caesar, in the name of racial, national, mental or physical superiority, usurps the place of God. In the closing years of a century which has been marred by barbaric contempt for human life and gross violations of human rights, Christians must 'obey God rather than men' in awakening consciences to the fundamental principle that 'from conception the weakest of persons has the right and duty to live.' To compromise on this principle is to unleash perverse forces which degrade our humanity and give rise to irrational violence.

In another key, it is clear that in ordinary linguistic usage the word 'person' evokes a reaction of respect or even reverence for the most precious beings encountered in our world. As Lustiger recalls, however, it was reflection on revelation, and specifically on the trinitarian communion of life and love in the divine nature, which gave rise to the concept of person. In the Christian perspective, then, a human person is constituted by a filial relationship with God rather than the possession of specified abilities and skills or the attainment of socially determined levels of perfection. Once more, it is a personal or I-Thou relationship between each human being and God which grounds the equal dignity of all members of the human family. While everyday experience shows that people are irredeemably unequal in various respects, neither mental nor physical deficiencies of whatever severity, nor differences of race, class or belief, warrant the withdrawal of an individual's right to the titles of 'person' and 'human being'. In the light of revelation every human being is a unique divine gift who is called to love and be loved. When individuals or societies yield to the temptation of Cain and transgress the commandment against murder, they defile the humanity which is common to us all. Yet, since the Bible is the 'memory of humanity', it can embrace all cultures and infuse them with its completely original and audacious personalism. To illustrate the transformation which is affected by the personalism of the Gospel, Lustiger cites a Slav prince's appreciation of the evangelising mission of Saints Cyril and Methodius: 'We who were ignored by everyone, were nothing. They came and gave us existence.' Lustiger is convinced that, as ancient Rome and the Slav territories were transformed by evangelisation, the cultural soil of the West can be irrigated again by the unique personalism of the Gospel.

Every generation in the Church's history is faced, of course, with the challenge of witnessing to the inexhaustible riches of Christian personalism. Lustiger sees Jean Vanier's *l'Arche* communities as beacons of light in societies which are often indifferent to the value of human lives. Inspired by the completely original personalism of the Gospel, these communities receive those who, according to prevailing criteria, are consigned to categories like 'the abnormal', 'the handicapped' or 'the marginalised' as persons equal in dignity, and in their weakness, salutary reminders of the wounds and short-comings of our own humanity. In *l'Arche* communities, we come to know the human condition through encounters with wounded brothers and sisters. We also learn of God's unrestricted love for every human being and of the vocation of each of us to love and be loved. Because the residents of *l'Arche* communities live the New Commandment and bear one anothers' burdens, they remind the Church and the world that God's power 'is manifested in weakness' and that the Suffering Servant 'became obedient unto death, even the death of the Cross'. The Christian truth about our humanity is also condensed for Lustiger in the reply of a Little Brother of Mother Teresa to his inquiry about the loving attention given to the 'outcasts' of the Paris metro: 'there is nothing that can be done for them; nothing, except to respect them and love them as they are'. But the original condensation of this truth is the disfigured face of Christ and 'the words of Pilate, spoken more truly than he realised, *Ecce Homo:* Behold *the* Human Being. Behold *Humankind.*'

Only Christians who love the Church, Lustiger insists, can be effective agents of evangelisation. To harbour resentment against the Church – or to pillory the sacramental and institutional dimensions of the Church – has to be seen as a form of spiritual suicide on the part of believers. Furthermore, animosity towards the Church signifies a forgetfulness of the fact that we all share in the history of guilt and that belief and conversion engage each of us in a lifelong struggle against our sinful and idolatrous inclinations. Nor can there be any place for the indulgent expectation of an ideal or 'invisible' Church distinct from the community of sinful believers who must always entrust themselves to God's mercy and hope for forgiveness and salvation. For Lustiger, the manner in which we treat the Church is the measure of our response to Christ. Rather than being a peripheral appendage to the mystery of salvation, the Church is the Body of Christ and continues to bear the wounds of human sinfulness in every age. As an institution, however, the Church must continually guard against the temptation of surrendering her specific identity – that of being, with and in Christ, 'a sign of contradiction' and a bearer of mercy, hope and salvation.

Despite the criticisms which have been directed against Christianity by the modern 'masters of suspicion' and the numerous attempts to consign faith to earlier unenlightened stages of human development or subsume it in prevailing ideologies, Lustiger has no hesitation in affirming that the passage of the centuries has not exhausted the riches of Christ and that the 'irreducible novelty' of Christian revelation emerges with ever greater clarity in the closing years of the second millennium. Rather than signalling the obsolescence of Christianity the uncertainty and insecurity of contemporary culture serve to highlight 'the unsurpassable truth of the Gospel'. Today, the timeless question – 'What gain, then, is it for a man to win the whole world and lose his soul, his life?' – provokes and demands a response as in earlier proclamations of the Gospel to Romans, Celts, Slavs and other peoples. Neither the spectacular scientific and technological advances, nor the idolatrous strands of our culture, can erode 'the eternal challenge of the Gospel which grounds human happiness on hope in the One who comes from Above'.

Christianity is also thoroughly realistic in its recognition and naming of evil, sin and death. Since salvation comes from the crucified Saviour whose outstretched arms extend mercy and forgiveness to all peoples, there is no place for facile optimism about the human condition. But however stark and oppressive the mystery of iniquity may be, Christianity continues to proclaim God's unrestricted love and mercy. Lustiger believes that, as the wounds of the post-Conciliar Church are being healed, Christianity 'is experiencing a new dawn' and that the Gospel seed is already growing into the Christian tree of the third millennium. Significantly, it is young people who are discovering and reclaiming the riches which have been abandoned by their elders.

A time which portrays itself as post-modern cannot be post-Christian when many young people are recovering a truth enunciated on French soil by the second-century theologian and martyr, Irenaeus of Lyons, and the twentieth-century surrealist poet, Guillaume Apollinaire: *Christus omnem novitatem attulit seipsum afferens*; *Seul en Europe tu n'est pas antique, ô Christianisme.*

NOTE

1   I have drawn on the following publications of Lustiger: *Osez croire, osez vivre: Articles, conférences, sermons, interviews 1981-1984* (Éditions Gallimard, Paris, 1986); *Le Choix de Dieu: Entretiens avec Jean-Louis Missika et Dominique Wolton* (Éditions de Fallois, Paris, 1987); *Dieu Merci, Les Droits de l'Homme: Articles, conférences, homélies, interviews 1984-1989* (Éditions Criterion, Paris, 1990); *Nous avons rendez-vous avec l'Europe* (Éditions Mame, Paris, 1991).

The following are available in English translations: *Dare to Live* translated by Maurice Couve de Murville (St Paul Publications, Slough, 1986); *Dare to Believe,* translated by Nelly Marans and Maurice Couve de Murville (St Paul Publications, Slough, 1986); *Choosing God – Chosen by God: Conversations with Jean-Marie Lustiger* translated by Rebecca Howell Balinski (Ignatius Press, San Francisco, 1991).

For de Lubac's account of the Christian resistance, see his *Mémoire sur l'occasion de mes écrits* (Culture et Verité, Namur, 1989), pp. 47-59; *Christian Resistance to Anti-Semitism: Memories from 1940-1944* translated by Sister Elizabeth Englund OCD (Ignatius Press, San Francisco, 1990).